How to Make Money by Selling Land

My Tips for Buying and Selling Small Rural Tracts for Profit

Written by Pat Porter

Contents

Why We Write These Land Books.

You know, the real estate category is very small within the overall Amazon book universe. And the rural real estate (land) niche is just a tiny speck tucked away in a corner of that category. I know I'm not going to be writing the next Harry Potter tome and selling millions of copies or be on some national best seller list. I can live with that.

My goal with these books – this will be the seventh one – has been to provide a source for good, easy-to-read, common sense information to support our industry. Land brokerage is a multi-billion dollar per year industry here in the United States. More and more people want to own a slice of heaven. I want to help them do it and to contribute all I can in support of the great industry that has supported me. These books are a humble attempt to help do just that.

So read, enjoy, think, learn, and pass it along.

Please check out all our land related books at my Amazon Author Page.

Our RecLand Talks video blog has lots of specific information about land management, hunting and the outdoors, and who we are at RecLand. Check it out at www.RecLand.net/recland-news. Keep in touch with us on social media at Facebook, Instagram, YouTube, LinkedIn, TikTok, and Twitter. Just search RecLand, RecLand Realty, or RecLand Talks.

Pat Porter

Introduction

Here's how it started. I was driving to look at a new property a client called me to list in north Louisiana. I was thinking that this 38-acre listing was right in the sweet spot for the size tracts that many people want for rural home sites in our region. I wondered if this tract could be bought at a price where we could improve it and make some money on it just like the…

Well, just like the last several tracts I had bought over the last year! I had bought, personally and occasionally with a couple of partners, 12 different deals just like this. Well, not identical deals in size and use, but similar in that they were smaller tracts ranging from 12 to 80 acres.

I'd never really considered looking at my buying and selling in a context of time and lumping all the deals together into information that I could pass along to others. But this was the idea I just had.

Why not talk about how I do it? Why not break down some of the steps I take? Why not explain the things I do to buy and sell a tract for profit? The bite-sized pieces of information could be useful to others who wanted to do the same.

I consider myself somewhat of an expert in the rural land brokerage business. I mean, heck…I do own and manage a large regional land brokerage dealing with millions of dollars in listings each year. I do know my way around most types of land tracts. I haven't, however, thought of myself as an expert land investor. Yes, I've been involved in the purchase and sale of thousands of acres – and all made money! – but that's just me doing what I do. An expert? No. Something to teach? Maybe.

So, here it is. My steps, thoughts, and actions on how I managed to buy and sell 12 different small tracts in about 18 months…all at a profit. There were two large deals – one over 1000 acres and another at almost 5000 acres – that I was also involved in at the same time. Those deals are different than the 12 I'll use for discussion here. Those deals require a different level of funding and knowledge that may be more than you want to tackle. So, for here, we'll focus on the 12 smaller tracts and see what we can learn.

The following chapters are written in a way that they can be plucked out and used as separate pieces of information that can provide a needed piece of guidance along your way. Absorb it all as a whole or pick and choose what you want.

Let's take a look.

Chapter 1 – What This Book is NOT

First of all, the 12 deals that I'll be referring to in this book are not the "get rich quick!" kind of stuff. I don't have any objections to getting rich quickly. I just think that it doesn't happen nearly as often as some writers and "buy my master program" guys say it does.

Second, there's no "make a million dollars on your first real estate transaction" late night infomercial schemes happening here, either. This is just day-in day-out, meat and potatoes kind of land deals. The tracts I bought in the 18-month period ranged from 12 to 80 acres. This is what I enjoy doing. This is really what it's all about in terms of this business. You do deals, you make a little money. You do more deals; you make a little more money. Sometimes you make more money than on other deals. Sometimes things don't go your way and you break even or even lose some money.

It takes a lot of deals and a lot of action to do well in this type business. That's what we try to do. To use baseball lingo: I'm not out trying to hit home every at bat. I'm trying to hit singles, doubles and the occasional beat-the-tag triple. I'm trying to just do deal after deal. I keep my head down, eyes forward, and work each deal as it comes and just let it all add up as we go.

So, if you're OK with a rolled-up sleeves kind of approach where you don't mind getting your hands dirty, let's get started.

Chapter 2 – Getting Started

Create Some Sources to Find Properties

The first thing to do is create some sources for locating land deals. You must find some properties that have the potential to be profitable deals.

"Well Pat, hey, that's easy for you. You're running RecLand Realty, a large regional land brokerage. You've got plenty of sources for land deals." I hear you. Sure, we have hundreds of listings each year in several states. We have had deals cross our plate that first showed up on the RecLand radar. But RecLand is not my source for deals.

I was able to do these 12 deals in that year and a half period because I started looking for land deals. I started putting more time, effort, and focus on finding them. Over the last couple years prior to that, I hadn't done near the number of deals that I've done lately. I was focused on a couple large deals our investment groups were in as well as growing RecLand. I wasn't doing near the number of personal, smaller land deals that I've just done...and am continuing to do. So just being in the industry, in the business, is not a sure-fire way to have land deals fall in your lap. It just doesn't happen that way. You've got to aggressively look for them.

The way I suggest you begin is to start turning over stones from your computer. Let Google do a lot of the leg work for you at the start. There will be plenty of actual leg work YOU will have to do soon enough.

Do some basic searches in your locale to see what's for sale. Start looking at pricing, areas, types of land for sale, etc. Just do some serious window shopping to start building some mental shelves to stack data information. Use national land sites like LandFlip.com where you can search and sort by state, county/parish, and size. State and regional companies you may be aware of will also have land listings that you'll need to start scanning. Just start looking and letting the general information saturate your mind.

This "drinking from a firehouse" approach will result in general pieces of useable data starting to stick in your mind. You'll begin to see ranges of asking prices, typical tract sizes, various asking prices based on land types, etc. This will suddenly show its value to you when one day, when you are pouring over listings, you see a tract that has an asking price below the general price points you've been seeing. This is a waving flag. Look closer. You'd be surprised how you can occasionally find something that has been priced according to a lower use but can be sold for a higher and better use. This is where you can take advantage of a deal. You will notice some tracts that have been on the market for a long time. These are often ripe for offers that trigger an impatient seller to just sell it and move on.

Both above scenarios are not a daily occurrence. But they do occur. They are a source of a deal here and there that you will get, and others will miss. It's a spoke on a wheel. And you are going to add more spokes.

Other Spokes:

1. **Real estate agents you know.** Just start telling them you are looking for small to mid-size undeveloped tracts. Tell them a general acreage size just to help them. No need to overwhelm them with your wish list of things. If you do, you'll just fade away into the ether of their forgetfulness. You'll also run the risk of sounding like you don't know what you're talking about and they'll forget you as soon as you're off the phone. Tell them to just set you up on their email alerts with certain acreage sizes in the area. You do the looking and sorting when they come in. Don't expect much here. It's just a spoke in the wheel. You'll likely do more deals from your own work with the other things listed below.

   Be sure to include land agents with brokerages that specialize in land as well as agents from area residential and commercial companies. The residential / commercial agents will have land listings in their MLS (multi listing service.)

2. **Your attorney and accountant.** If you're in the line of work where you have relationships with these type professionals already, be sure to let them know you'd be interested in any rural properties they may hear about. These people are in positions where real estate discussions frequently occur, and deals are made between clients that are never listed and advertised.

3. **Local newspapers and online shoppers' guides.** People still put classifieds in print newspapers and discount shopper guides. A lot of real estate is sold by owner and never listed. Places like Penny Saver and Thrifty

Nickle magazines (or their equivalent in your area,) Craig's List, Facebook, etc. can all churn up possibilities.

4. **Other friends.** Do you have any friends or acquaintances that are foresters, farmers or ranchers, contractors, large equipment operators or salesmen, chemical or seed salesmen, mortgage brokers, veterinarians? Do you go to church with anyone who has a lawn service or mulching business? Do your kids play ball with someone who's dad owns a store that sells hardware, outdoor gear, lumber, landscape supplies, etc. You probably get my point.

   And before you rebut me with, "Pat, if they knew of anyone with anything good to sell, they'd buy it themselves." No, sir, that's not true. Very few people have the knowledge, ambition, desire, and resources to buy, improve, and sell rural real estate. Let people know you're looking. Bait that hook.

5. **Driving around.** Keep your eyes open to For Sale signs when you're on the road. This relates to number 3 above. Calling people who are selling their property without using a real estate agent will lead to deals. It's simply a matter of when, not if.

   Be sure to notice old barns and homes that are not being used or lived in. Look for gates with weeds and vines growing over them. These are signs that a property is just not as important to someone as it once was and may be an opportunity to buy with some of the tools in number 6 below.

6. **Use the public records.** This is a little more advanced than the others. It will soon be a regularly used tool, however, if you continue working to buy and sell land. Learning to look up property owners and reach out to them by letter or telephone is a great tool to acquiring property. I use public records almost daily in my work as both a broker and an investor. We can't get into it here but know that you'll want to start understanding how to access data from your County Recorder of Deeds, Parish Clerk of Court, District Clerk, Appraisal District, Assessor's Office, etc.

Getting started means developing many possible sources. It means beginning the never-ending process of studying land, prices, uses, etc. in the geography where you want to buy and sell so you are honing a good working knowledge of what a deal will look like when you find one. Getting started requires turning over a lot of stones. It requires planting a lot of seeds. It will take time and diligence. It will take follow-up and hustle. Don't expect things to fall in your lap if you're not putting forth any effort. But do expect to swerve into things from time to time if you are buyt looking!

Define Your Geography

We brushed by this a little in the previous section about creating sources. It's important that you have some general idea of the geography you want to focus on. You will need to set some boundaries to make the best use of your time and resources. You want to have a general area that you know you can get around in to look at tracts, make trips to it to work or follow up on people like surveyors.

Since we're talking about rural real estate and not houses. Your geography may be several counties whereas your residential investor friend may have an area that is a couple for subdivisions south of the loop. The point is, know where you want to focus – at least initially until you've done several deals – and be laser focused there. This will help you get market values bracketed in your mind much easier, too.

Determine Your Financial Field

"Hey! I know about 4800 acres for sale just 2 hours from you!" Uh...OK...but can you swing 4800 acres? Do you have a group who can quickly put together a deal like that? If not, don't get blinded by the undoable. Knowing where you are financially in your plan to invest in rural real estate keeps you focused. Making the main thing the main thing is the...well...the main thing!

We can't get into detailed finances here. You bought this book. You're a smart person. You understand generally what league you're playing in when you decide to try to buy 60 acres of timberland in your area. You'll know what I mean by determining your financial field. You know you must have coins to play this game.

Let me outline a few things to get you thinking and then you determine where you are and how many "coins" you want to set aside to play.

1. Most deals are easier if you are a cash buyer or have access to cash in a line of credit.

2. Financing rural real estate is not difficult. It will typically require 15-20% down in cash, good financial records

showing a lender your ability to repay, 1-3 years of tax returns, and a deal that has enough upside to offset the costs of financing (actual expenses and the time it takes to repay that will result in interest expense.)

3. If you are a cash buyer, then this amount is your budget. It's your financial field. It's well defined. If you have some cash that you will use in a financing deal, then keep in mind that 15-20% down is probably a minimum. You may also want to get some 3rd party help to be sure you understand how to project your costs over time if you're not experienced in how interest will chip away – daily! – at your potential profit until it then begins chipping away at your down payment.

4. Go talk with your lender about your plans and get some general guidance from them. Some lenders are not used to rural real estate and you may want to start investigating who in your area understands it well and is seeking that type lending business. I assure you not all lenders are created equally! The bank that financed your house or boat may be the last one you'd want to try to use to help you with 40 acres.

Ask Yourself a Hard Question

Do you really want to do this? It must be more than: "Buying and selling land…sounds like fun! I think I'll try it."

There must be some deep interest in this, or you'll fizzle out. It will prove to be hard work. It will demand a lot of time. It's a financial risk. Sometimes, it's a long time between deals. This means the action of buying and selling stops, but the work doesn't. Do you really want to do this?

I do three things in my life. One, I run RecLand. It's a regional real estate brokerage specializing in selling hunting land, timberland, farms, and ranches in six states. Two, I hunt – primarily bow hunt for deer. I duck and turkey hunt when I can. And three, I raise my family. That's it. Two of those three things, and the third indirectly, all keep me in the world of rural real estate. Yea...I'm interested enough to keep at it even when it gets hard. Are you?

Chapter 3 – Solving Problems

One way to make money on real estate is to buy it at a price lower than the actual value. You then just resell it at market value and make the gross profit of the difference between purchase price and sales price. Easy, right? Sure. It happens like that occasionally. A couple of the deals in the 12 that are the basis for this book were just like that.

I purchased a 20-acre wooded tract in a remote area of southcentral Missouri for about $400-500 / acre less than what I believed it could easily sell for. The owner was asking a little less than what I thought the market value was. I offered a few hundred dollars an acre less than that. We negotiated to a cash deal. I sold it 3 months later for a gross profit of about $8500 without doing anything to it other than listing it with a good land agent in Missouri and letting him sell it.

There are two things to note here. One, I told you this was not a "get rich quick" scheme! This was simply a 20-acre rural timberland deal with a quick few thousand dollars in profit. Two, the deal was a money maker simply by purchasing it at a wholesale price and reselling at retail. There was no work to be done. No zoning committee had to be applied to. I didn't have to hire a surveyor, pay a bulldozer operator, or buy an easement for access.

These are deals you just get by paying attention and learning general market values like we discussed in the last chapter. The value (profit) was already built in the deal with the purchase price.

Other deals, however, don't have the value already in place because of the purchase price. You must build the value in some way. One way to do that is to solve a problem.

Sometimes you're able to make good deals on a property, because you're able to solve problems that other people cannot or will not solve. You may be able to overcome costly challenges on a tract that other people can't, not just because you have more money than someone else. You may have more resources, more time, more information, or just more determination to stick with something until it gets solved. Solving problems on a piece of real estate is usually the way to turn a so-so deal for everybody else into a good deal for you.

One problem I solved on three of the 12 deals here was securing a deeded, legal access to tracts that were being sold without a deeded access. We won't get into deeded easements and servitudes here. I've written about it in some of my other books like "More Land Buying Tips from the Pros" and have talked about it a number of times in some of our YouTube videos at the RecLand Talks channel.

A property that doesn't front a public road, or have a deeded access to a public road, will typically sell for less than the same tract with legal, public road access. If you are able to solve the access problem where others could not or would not, you will likely have an opportunity for a deal. I was able to do this on three occasions in an 18-month period. Each time we were able to make several hundred dollars an acre on the tracts.

Other problems that you may can solve that others cannot or will not:

1. Being able to build roads in and through a tract because you have the equipment due to other work you already do. Or, you can rent the equipment and operate it proficiently yourself. Either way, you add value to the tract at less cost than other people who don't have those resources.

2. You have friends who can partner with you in the deal who are logging contractors, surveyors, irrigation specialists, adjacent landowners, mulching machine owner / operator, fencing company owner, etc. In each case, you can solve potential problems on a property cheaper, faster, and easier because you have the "resources" others don't have.

3. Be willing to clear up title issues like an undivided interest. This is almost a whole book itself. But in a nutshell, an undivided interest, also called a tenancy in common in most states, is when several people all own a percentage of a property, but only on paper and by virtue of math. They haven't divided up the property according to their interest. It's like you, me, and two of my friends all owning a pie. We may all have 25% each, but which slice is your 25%? Which slice is my 25%? Just slice it up and problem solved, right? Wrong! Sure, it's easy to equally slice a pie, but how do you equally slice 300 acres?

   No, it's not just math. The acres aren't the same as are the slices of pie. Some of the 300 acres join a highway with available utilities. Some of the acres have pine timberland. Some of the acres are in a boggy, wet slough ½ mile from the road. Everyone owns a percentage of that 300 acres, but who gets what? That's the issue.

Being willing to secure all the parties' ownership percentages in an undivided interest scenario is often a big money maker. We have done it several times...including the 300 acres scenario where there were 33 heirs and took a little over a year! It's not one of the 12 deals I refer to here, and it was several years ago. It was, however, a good example of solving a problem others would not or could not tackle.

This will require some help from a title attorney to clearly identify all the owners and their respective percentages of ownership. It will also take a steady effort over time. Sometimes, you'll get a lot of "no way!" on the first, second, and third attempts. Sticking with the project over time is usually the key. This is why most people will never tackle this.

4. Having the ability to put together money is a way to solve a problem on a larger tract or one that is expensive due to location and use. Some properties just don't sell well because few people can easily come up with the money. Having the ability to put together an investment group easily and quickly can sometimes be the key to a great deal.

    This is not a tool that was used on any of these 12 deals because they were all modest in size. I have put together deals on large tracts simply because we had a fast-moving group who could cash out an impatient seller. The size of the deal was the main problem. The quick access to a flexible investor group was the solution. I mention it here because this may be where some of you end up as you do more deals and have more opportunities in the future.

There is really no end to the number of possibilities that you could put on the table regarding potential issues and their needed solutions, and then having friends, family members, and partners who can bring the resources to bear to provide those solutions. That's a good way to look at tracts. Figure out what the problem is and why it is the way it is. If you can solve it, would that make that property more valuable? If so, can you solve it at a reasonable price to be able to then take that piece of property and do what you want to do with it to make the money you want to make, or for it to be the type of property you want to keep for yourself? Solving problems is a step to making good real estate deals.

This same principle could apply to houses and commercial buildings. Solving major problems that are tripping everybody else up is a potential place to make some money on any type of real estate.

Chapter 4 – Learn to Pull the Trigger

This piece of advice I want to pass along popped in my head soon after I got a text from a title company telling me they had a set a closing date for a 40-acre deal. This was one of the 12 deals this book is about.

I found that 40 acres by simply turning over stones. We discussed looking for deals in Chapter 2.   Sometimes you find stuff and when you're doing work - turning over stones. You occasionally swerve into things you weren't necessarily looking for. You may find a deal just because you're out looking for something else. Good things can happen when you work hard and you're hustling and looking.

Well, this deal came along like that. I was looking at tracts and a gentleman called me I had help with some properties in the past. He said, "Pat, hey, we have a couple tracts we just need to get sold. Can you go look at them?" I said, "Sure."

Long story made short...I ended up making a deal on one of them. It was a nice little 40-acre tract. Not big. Just a nice little deal.

The point I want to make is if you're going to do this, at some point, you must get to a place where you're ready to pull the trigger. "Pull the trigger" is just a way of saying fish or cut bait, get in or get out. You can't analyze a deal six ways from Sunday over and over. You can't think of every little minute thing and get it down to where there's absolutely no risk, no chance of anything going wrong. You can't always wait for the perfect time – whatever that is.

Some deals are much better than others and you get all the signals pointing at go. And there are other deals that you're getting mixed signals or obvious red flags on. I understand that sometimes the decision is crystal clear what you should do. But sometimes, it's not a definite yes or no. You just know it's just a reasonable deal with no apparent pitfalls. If everything goes the way you have it planned out, you should make a little money. It doesn't have to go perfectly. It just needs to proceed along a reasonable course, in a reasonable market, in a reasonable time, and you'll be able to make a little money, and you can buy the tract without using next month's house note or car payment to do it.

The risk is low. You got a good chance of making some money. It fits what you do. You're not getting in over your head. It's not something that's completely new to you, or a different type of tract in different location where there are a lot of variables that you don't have answers to a lot of questions. It just looks like a good, solid deal.

You gotta pull the trigger! You have to get to a point where you say, "Hey, it's all lining up. Let's just do it." Now don't misunderstand me and take this as me saying, "You should rush into a deal." Never rush into a deal. Never go against your gut. Never go against all the red flags. You don't want to make a bad deal. One bad deal will set you way back. It'll take you a long time just to get back to where you are, especially when you're doing things on a shoestring with a modest stash of resources. You can't afford to make a bad deal.

However, when everything is telling you, "Hey, it's a good, solid deal. It may not be the sexiest deal in the world, but it's a good solid standup double kind of deal." - to use a little baseball metaphor - sign it up and go do it. Get it done.

The way I look at a lot of deals is just like the way I explained it recently to a client. He was looking at a hundred acres that joins a big tract that I helped him buy. We were looking at it and he started analyzing it to death and micro-tearing it apart. Finally, I said, "You know, at X price, you can't get hurt." "You can't get hurt" is my way of saying, "Just do the deal at this number." If you can buy it for this number, you can't get hurt. You're not going to mess up. You might not make a lot of money, but you're not going lose any money, either.

So, when you find yourself at a place looking at tracts, doing all your due diligence, and you're in that, "I can't get hurt," kind of place, go ahead and pull the trigger. Chances are, if you've done good due diligence, if you've done your homework, you'll likely make money. The deal's going to turn out at least as good, maybe even better than you thought. At the worst, however, you can't get hurt.

And consider this. Even of you do spend a lot of time on a marginal deal, or even lose a little bit of money because everything seemed to go wrong, you're still going to come out ahead. Here's why - because you got in a deal. Things didn't work out. This went wrong and that went wrong. You lose a little bit of money or just barely break even. Don't forget. You still learned a world of information.

People discount the things they learn in doing deals that is so valuable. That information you learned in the bad deal may be the very thing that makes you a bunch of money or keeps you from getting in a deal where you were going lose a bunch of money on the next deal. So just because you don't see it in a check at a closing doesn't mean that you didn't get something out of a deal.

To sum it all up, when you find yourself in that, "Hey, everything looks good, can't get hurt, about 92% sure" kind of deal, and you have the money and time, pull the trigger and make the deal. See what happens. Learn something.

You'll probably make some money. When you look back on it you'll go, "Ah, I'm glad I did that!" It will strengthen your instincts. When you act on your instincts and then see those instincts play out it makes you trust your instincts even more going forward.

That's not so important on the good things, but it is critical when your instincts are telling you to run, telling you to get away, telling you, "Don't get into that deal or do business with that person." Your instincts, in my opinion, are more useful to keep you out of bad situations than getting you into good ones.

Good common sense, due diligence, information, using the sense God gave, and working hard will get you in good deals. Good instincts can keep you out of bad deals. Trust your gut. Pull the trigger. Make some deals.

Chapter 5 – Quiz the Neighbors

As you can imagine, I look at a lot of property. I drive a pickup that has my company information on it in a very cool and colorful wrap. I'm hard to miss and it's difficult for me to be inconspicuous when I'm driving down the road or on a piece of property somewhere.

I was recently looking at three 40s in Arkansas. Each one was on a road that seemed to have a lot of houses on it for the rural area I was in. I had to park close to houses to get into a couple of these 40's. My habit is, when I do that, I go knock on the door that's closest to where I'm parking, or the one that's closest to the tract. I do this just to let somebody know what I'm doing. I tell them, "Hey, I'm back here looking at this piece of property for the owner." That's what I'm doing and that's the truth. I continue with, "I just wanted you to know so you wouldn't think somebody's out here doing something stupid." That's my typical line. They laugh and are often appreciative. I've never had a problem, ever, doing that. And I ask them, "Is it okay if I leave my truck here?" People are more than happy to help. I've never had an issue.

I did that on two of these Arkansas tracts. I went up to the front door and knocked. I always back away from the door and I try to look kind of humble and goofy, because I'm a big guy with a big beard, so I try not to be intimidating. As soon as they come to the door, I always say, "Hey, my name is Pat Porter. I'm not trying to sell you anything." I always try to disarm people so that they don't have any reason to be nervous. Both houses where I knocked had elderly ladies answering the doors. They were somebody's grandmothers and great-grandmothers. The last thing I wanted to do was cause them to feel alarmed.

So anyway, "Hey, I'm Pat Porter. I'm not selling anything. I just wanted to tell you what I'm doing." And I tell them why I'm there.

Well, both of these different tracts, with two different ladies, both sweet little old ladies, ended up giving me a lot of information about the property that was joining them. Once they initiated some talk about the land I was looking at, I felt comfortable to ask other general questions that helped me learn about the area. They had lived there a long time. I got some information on access. I got some information on a boundary dispute on one of the tracts. I received a lot of little tidbits on the parcels, simply just by being a nice guy and introducing myself to the neighbors and letting them know that I was there. Just doing the courteous thing, I got some good information on these properties.

I've done that so many times because it's just the right thing to do. And by doing this I have gotten mountains of good information on properties I've looked at that I might not have gotten any other way. This kind of information helps you understand things that can influence the resell of the tracts you buy.

Don't be afraid to knock on doors or to introduce yourself to people that may have some connection or some type of involvement in or around a piece of property you're looking at.

They may know some previous owners. They may know some family members. They may know some adjoining neighbors that there's information that you can use to help you in deciding if it's a deal you want to do, because sometimes neighbors are an important factor in some deals.

Being humble and being stupid goes a long way sometimes! I try to be sweet and stupid when I'm talking to people and let them tell me what they want to tell me. We walk away after shaking hands. You've made a new friend. That's just a good way to do business in my opinion. So, don't be afraid to talk to people.

One little caveat. Keep in mind if this is the type of deal or situation that you may not want anybody to know that you're looking at the tract. If that's the case for me, I try to just be in and out quietly. I'll be as discreet as possible. I'll go park somewhere else so that I can walk in a long way and just try to keep my business my business at that point because I don't want people to know what I'm looking at. I don't want people to know my client's business.

Just consider the situation. Is it okay for people to know what I'm doing out there? If it is, knock on doors and politely ask general questions. Let them talk. You just listen. If you're trying to be discreet, you may have to park somewhere and walk in a long way or cut across a creek bottom or something else to get to where you need to be.

I think you get the point. Asking questions is vital in making good land deals or good real estate deals of any kind. Of course, there are many places where you'll ask questions in your due diligence work. You'll certainly be talking with tax assessors, surveyors, attorneys, real estate agents, engineers, utility companies, dirt contractors, foresters and loggers, drainage commissions, farm service agencies, etc. But I wanted to make clear the necessity of talking to as many neighbors as you can, too. The conversations will be less formal, but the information may be the best you get!

Chapter 6 – Buying Without Seeing

Maybe you've done a deal or two. Maybe you're just getting started and have never done a deal. You may be a pro who has dozens of deals under your belt. Regardless of where you are along the experience spectrum, sooner or later you'll have the opportunity of buying a piece of property sight unseen.

I gave some thought to just typing the word "DON'T!" under the chapter heading and going to chapter 7. But that would be a little cheesy. Even though I strongly recommend you do not do it, the fact is that I've done it. It's the ol' "exception to the rule" thing, I guess.

Let's talk about it just a little deeper. What got me to thinking about addressing this is I see stuff on the internet all the time about "how to buy land cheap," or "cheap land in Arizona", or "cheap land here," or "owner finance," or "we finance your lot here." It's just enticing people or playing on people's desire to own a piece of property, to own land, somewhere, anywhere. They try every way they can to make it seem like it's a simple, cheap, painless, easy, risk-free process. Nothing could be further from the truth. If it sounds too good to be true, you know the adage, it most likely is.

As far as your looking for land and trying to do land deals, I absolutely recommend against buying something sight unseen.

Here are some exceptions.

1. If you have tons of information. I mean information from reliable people, not the information from the people who are trying to sell it. Not that the people trying to sell it aren't reliable, but my point is they have a dog in the race. You need information from people who don't have any kind of skin in the game. They just are providing the information from a third-party, arms-length position. and it's just they don't have any reason to sort of sway you one way or the other. You need good information.

2. You must have the ability to handle some risk. You need the ability to be able to lose some money. So, if you're scraping under the couch cushions for the last piece of change to make a deal, you definitely don't need to make it on a deal that's got a lot of risk. Buying a tract sight unseen has more risk. Make sure you can handle the risk if you choose to do that. Make sure you've got as much information as you can gather.

3. You need to have a specific plan in place prior to purchasing. We'll talk more about planning in another chapter, but when you buy a tract sight-unseen, you need to have the long-distance managing in place as well as your exit strategy.

4. You must still have some knowledge about the area even though you've never seen the tract. It must still be in your wheelhouse, so to speak, with regard to the type of property it is and the locale in which you'll be trying to resell it.

One of the 12 deals I've referred to in the premise of this book was in another state. I bought it without ever seeing it. Keep in mind, it wasn't just a blind, throwing a dart in the dark kind of deal. I had a lot of good information. It was in a state that we're licensed in. RecLand does business there. It was a piece of property that one of my land agents in that state had listed. The seller just wanted to sell it. He was lowering the price to the point that I asked myself, "Well, doggone, is there a deal to be made here?"

I called my land agent up there and started asking questions about the tract. He's not a seasoned land pro, but he has good sense. He knows the area. He knows the recreational potential of a piece of property like that. He's a great deer hunter himself. He knows what to look for in a piece of property that he's interested in, as far as the recreational value. So, I knew that the information I was getting from him was good information. I put all the pieces of the information together and said, "Well, shoot, there's just not much risk here." It was only 20 acres. It was not going to bust the bank if I messed up. I pulled the trigger. See chapter 4!

Everything was just pointing to the fact that it was a comfortable deal in terms of the risk versus reward. I had information. I had a plan. I had the money. I bought it without seeing it.

I quickly put the tract back on the market and sold it. It was a decent little deal. It didn't make a lot of money. I mean, how much money can you make on a 20-acre rural tract, anyway? It's not like it was 20 acres of development property in the middle of Dallas. It was a 20-acre recreational tract in the Midwest. We bought it sight unseen. There were no problems. It was a quick, easy deal. It worked out just like it was supposed to.

That was a success story. But for every success story when buying something sight unseen, there's probably many stories where the people would say, "Don't do it!" Everything went wrong. They didn't have good information. They didn't have workable plans. They didn't have the ability to get things done from long distance. They weren't seasoned pros. They likely got more emotionally attached to just making a deal so that they didn't really take the risk into consideration, and that happens. Believe me, I understand that. I've made mistakes on land deals where I was so caught up in the deal that I ignored all the red flags that I tell people to watch for. I talk about that in one of my other books, Land Mines.

With that said, avoid deals that are sight unseen unless you trust the party on the ground where that tract is who are your eyes and are passing that information back to you. If you got a guy standing on the ground telling you about the tract, and you can trust him and you know his base of experience and knowledge and understanding of deals, you've got a better chance. If you're doing it completely on your own, trusting somebody who's trying to just sell it to you, and no matter how easy they make the deal in terms of owner financing, or terms, or anything like that, stay away from those until you have more experience under your belt.

I know it's not encouraging to tell you to avoid these type deals, because you want an easy way to make deals and you might not be currently finding any where you are right now. And then suddenly you hear about one way out yonder in another region of a country. It sounds great! I understand the feeling. I'm just encouraging you to calm down, slow down, relax, don't rush it, don't push it, and just say no to those deals until you learn to do some deals there in your home territory.

Chapter 7 – Making Offers

Let's talk about making offers. No, this isn't going to be a Trumpian level discussion of the Art of the Deal. That's great for the high-level, fast paced, multi-million-dollar projects that he does. My approach to negotiating and making offers is simple. I'll tell you exactly what I do, and I'll tell you what some other people do. But in the end, you do what works for you.

Our discussion here will be more about philosophy than technique. Once you know your philosophy, you can create a few little practical steps – techniques – to help you carry it out in your offers to buy property.

At the end of the day, no matter how you make offers and negotiate a deal, you need to do it the way it fits your personality. If you try to be something you're not, or if you're using a technique, people notice. It jumps out. I see it all the time.

People regularly call and talk to me and deal with me on properties. It could be our listings or stuff that we own personally. I can always tell when they're running a scam. I don't mean running a scam in a way that they're trying to be dishonest. They're just going down the most recent sales and objections list that they've read in a negotiation book. That has its place. My point is that it's not genuine. It's not sincere, and it comes off like that. Whatever you do, do it in a way that fits your personality. Here's what I do.

First, I always have an exit strategy in mind before I make an offer on a tract to try to buy it. I have an idea of what it ought to resell for, and with that in mind, I have an idea of what I'd like to buy it for. I try to buy a tract in a range that we can make a good return. Now that's not an exact, set, firm number on every deal. It varies deal to deal. We try to make a good, fair return on a deal. Sometimes we hit a home run and do much better than we ever thought. Other times, we eke out a little profit and move on to the next one. But we always have a plan of how much we realistically want to make on a deal.

Next, I go into the deal trying to buy it somewhere around my, "I just want this plan to work" number. I don't go in trying to steal a deal. That's slang for buying it at some absurdly low number. That works for some people. It doesn't work for me because it takes too much time. You get shot down more times than it's successful, and I don't have time for that. I want to make a deal and move on.

I make realistic offers. I make the offer based on, "I need to buy it for this so I can sell it for that to make a fair profit." If I can do that, great. If I can't, I move on. I don't spend a lot of time tearing a tract down, talking about all the negatives to try to get them to come down off their price. I make an offer. I tell them what my thinking is in a couple of sentences and just be straight-forward about it. That's my personality though.

I just make it clear what my positions is. There's not a whole lot of going back and forth. They may counter, and I may counter a little bit. We'll make the deal, or we don't. My point is I go into it with a number in mind I want to buy it for, a number in mind I want to sell it for, and if I can buy it around that number, I say, "Sign it up. Let's move on."

I've explained it this way to other partners and friends of mine. I kind of have a "circle" or range. If we the purchase price gets somewhere in that circle, I'll make the deal. It doesn't have to be to the far low side of that circle or range for me to make the deal. No. It might be on the middle or the high side. If it's in that circle, sign me up. Let's quit wasting time discussing it trying to save another $20 an acre. If it's close, sign it up. Done deal.

I know there are people who fight and claw for every nickel in a deal. That's them. That's not me. I am all for a win-win. It doesn't have to be an "I win more" for me to do the deal.

If it's in the circle, sign it up. That doesn't work for everybody. "Pat, I can get some more out of that deal." They can squeeze and squeeze and maybe get someone to sell lower. We've got a friend who's just that way. We joke with him all the time. He'd spend an hour on the phone negotiating to save 10 cents on a knob on an electric stove. He's just that kind of guy. I'm not that kind of guy. "Hey, how much is the knob?" "Well, it's 75 cents." "I'll take it." Not our friend though. He'll stay at it and negotiate it down to 65 cents. I'm not that guy. He is. He does very well with that because it fits his personality.

I make an offer somewhere in the range that I need to buy it at and if we make a deal, great. If we don't, I move on. Other people go in and low ball like my buddy and try to get the seller down as far as he can go. I don't do that. I don't like when I get low balled. Low balling doesn't work for me. It turns most people off and I don't have the personality to pull it off. I'm kind of straightforward. What you see is what you get, and if I were to come in with a really low-ball offer, it just is phony as it can be because that's just not me.   Go about it however it suits you.

I hate getting in these kinds of situations where somebody feels they have got to scalp the other person for it to be a win to them.

It happens all the time. People do it. They're made up that way. It's not me. It must be a win/win or I'm not comfortable with it.

If somebody approaches me and I can tell that it's a win or die kind of thing for them, where they're the only ones who are going to come out in the deal, I say to heck with them. I don't care if I miss a deal. I'm not going to do business with people like that. I don't like it. I don't enjoy it. I don't pretend to. I try to negotiate with people the way I'd want them negotiating with me.

Some people make offers by really having a tight plan and going in with their best number. They know exactly what they want to buy it for. They make the offer…which is often a pretty solid number. It is either accepted or rejected by the seller. They either take the deal, with the buyer's best offer, or the buyer just moves to the next one. I've seen this work well for some people. The downside, in my opinion, is that most people feel some back and forth must occur. This approach leaves no room for that dynamic.

I prefer to go in with a number that leaves me some room to come up if the seller makes a counteroffer. I've had people accept my first offer, which is always a nice surprise. But I always leave some room for me to come up yet still be within my plan's range or circle.

One thing I don't do is that nonsense where I come up $5 an acre or $100 lump sum. Some people counter like that. It drives me insane dealing with $3500 or $5000 an acre stuff and somebody moves $5 or $10 an acre. We see it all the time negotiating deals between clients with RecLand. It's absurd in my opinion. I guess some people have more time on their hands. But I make a realistic offer, hope to get a good counteroffer, and then if I need to move a little bit to try to make the deal, I do. I move once or twice and it either happens or it doesn't. That's me. Other people go in with the low-ball and then go up $5, $10 until they just make the other party mad and lose the deal – a deal they may could have gotten by just being reasonable and settling for a win-win.

If you're that gung-ho shark, that low-ball guy who's going to go out there and try to steal one out of a hundred deals by going in there at such a low-ball number, knock yourself out if that's you. I'm not going to enjoy doing business with you. Most people aren't. Your mama doesn't even like that. I'm sorry. I didn't mean to bring your mama into it. My point is, if that's you, do what you do. Other people are more businesslike and try to make a win-win deal. There are people who don't like the process at all. They don't like the back and forth at all. I have a really good client who hates that process. He understands it's the nature of the beast. He gets me to negotiate his deals because he knows that most people need to go back and forth a little bit. He's recognized his personality that he doesn't like doing that, and he doesn't want to get in a bad deal.

Find out what works for you. Do your homework, have a plan, and make your offer based on that plan. And stick to your plan!

One of my best friends and a business partner is a sharp businessman. He has said the following a thousand times: "It's better to miss 10 good deals than to make 1 bad deal."

That is so true because you use up a lot of your bullets on a bad deal, it takes a long time to recover. So, know when to walk away.

Know when a deal is starting to get outside the range of your plan and is just not going to work. Don't fall in love with it so much that you keep chasing it. You'll end up chasing it outside the range of your plan. You'll end up buying a piece of property for more than you knew you should have because you got so tied up in it emotionally or just wanting to do a deal or trying to impress somebody. Whatever the reason, do not to chase a deal.

We all have done that at some point. If you already have, don't feel bad. It happens sometimes. Just let it be a good lesson learned. Have your number in your mind and be disciplined enough to not chase after a deal once it gets outside your circle.

Pro tip: You don't have to come back with an answer right away when the seller makes a counteroffer! One thing I've learned from some other people is it's okay to say, "Hey, let me think on it awhile and I'll get back with you."

You might know exactly what you're going to say, exactly what you want to do, but just simply creating a little cushion of time between what was last said in the deal and the next thing that is said may provide an advantage. Sometimes, things happen during those cushions of times that change the deal. Use a cushion of time to think as an honest technique. It may be nothing more than taking time to walk outside, drink a Coke, stare at the clouds for an hour or so before you go back inside, or you call the guy on the phone and give him your answer or your number. At least you've thought about it a little and you haven't appeared to be so anxious.

Taking a little time always creates some sense of urgency with the seller who is secretly wanting to make the deal with you. I don't have exact numbers on this, but I'd venture to guess that about 1 in 5 times the seller has called back to say he'd go ahead and take my last offer. Some sellers are ready to make a deal and move on, but they feel like they have to keep nibbling to get more. If you stop the process, they feel like the opportunity to get more has ended, and they sometimes make the deal. Your cushion of time works on both sides of the deal!

One last thought about this win-win approach. Chances are you are going to have to do more than one deal in this life to make any money. You're likely not going to hit this multi-million-dollar home run your first time out buying 20 acres. Regardless of what the other guy said in his course or book, you're just not going to do it. You must do a lot of deals. The world gets small when you're buying and selling land. It gets even smaller when you try to do win-lose deals as opposed to win-win. Word gets around. Lives and stories intersect. Your reputation will proceed you – good or bad. I'd like to think you and I would want to do deals with the same person again if the opportunity presented itself. Don't ruin tomorrow's deals by being a win-lose guy today.

Chapter 8 – Have an Exit Plan

I typically have a very specific plan for each tract I buy including those bought during this period. I didn't just think, "Well, maybe I'll just buy them, and something will work out." I had very specific reasons for purchasing them…a plan. That's the thing I wanted to focus on here…having a plan.

That sounds so elementary. "Oh, of course, Pat. I never would buy a piece of land without a plan." You'd be surprised how many people do. They really don't have an exit strategy thought out before they get neck deep in all the details of buying something. I had a detailed plan for each of these tracts long before I made the offer. I already had the thing formulated in my head exactly how it would work out, and the only thing that I didn't know during that planning time was if I'd be able to buy the tracts at what I wanted to buy them for to fit my plan.

Let's use two small tracts I bought in Texas as examples here. One was 12 acres. One was 15 acres. Fortunately, I was able to buy both tracts right about where I thought I'd be able to buy them, so my plan was off to a good start. Hopefully, it was a good plan, and It would all work out.

The 15-acre tract was landlocked, had good pine sawtimber, and joined another tract that we already owned. The reason I wanted to buy the 15 acres was to add it to this other tract that we were going to have the timber cut. I could now have both tracts cut at the same time. Having more timber volume on a logging job makes it better for the logger (he can set up in one location and cut and haul timber without having to relocate) and you can get slightly better prices, preferential treatment, or both.

Part two of the plan is that I was already securing a legal access to the tract I owned. Now, by buying the adjoining 15-acre tract, my cost for the access gets spread out over a bigger tract. At the end of the day, I'm taking a good deal and making it a much better deal by adding to it. I'm adding to it at a price that I know we can make money. My cost for access to the original tract was going to be about $8,000. My cost will still be about $8000, but now it's an improvement cost benefitting more acres. It just works out all the way around. It's a good plan.

The 12-acre parcel accomplishes part of the same thing the 15-acre tract did. It adds acreage to a tract we already owned. The 12 acres was landlocked. Our tract had access. By adding the 12 acres to our bigger tract, we were also giving it legal access. That's a big improvement and adds value. We were also going to have some trails made on the tract we owned to help improve it for recreational use. Now we'll just add a few hours to the mulcher or dozer job to improve the added 12 acres and improve a bigger tract for just a little extra money. Buying that 12 acres made us money the minute we closed. It was a good plan.

My point in all this is when you see a piece of ground you like, and you're thinking, "Hey, the price looks good and so I could buy it well. There may be some money to be made here." Be sure to think through your exit strategy, your plan. Have your exit strategy already planned out before you even get into trying to buy. Knowing how you're going to get out is a lot more important than knowing how to get in. I suggest reading that last sentence again!

There are some deals out there that are such a sweet deal that you could buy it and figure it out later. We've done that because it was just such an incredible deal, but for the most part, the only way to know it's a good deal is to know how you're going to get out of it in a reasonable time period and reasonable cost. Have your exit plan in place before you even start getting into the deal.

Also, be prepared for your exit plan to change. One of the tracts that's on this list of 12 that I've got going is an example. I had a good, detailed exit plan in place. Before we even closed on it, my plan got changed to a better plan. It's just one of those times when if you do enough deals and you got enough activity going, you're turning over enough stones, sometimes good things happen. The bottom line was I spoke to an adjoining landowner about our plans and he wanted to just buy the place from us without our having to do anything. It was at a price where we could make good money with no effort, no improvement cost, no interest, no property taxes to pay, and no additional time. That wasn't my plan, but it was a better deal!

Have a detailed plan. Think through what you want to do with the property. Think through different scenarios. Have a, "Hey, I can do this or I can do that" approach. They may make different amounts of money. They may have different time spans as to how long it takes each plan to work but give yourself some outs. Those of you who play poker, you know what I'm talking about. You're holding cards and you see the flop, you got some different outs – ways to make a good hand. You need outs in the land business. It's hard to put all your eggs in one little basket and hope that everything works out just right. You need some good plans, some solid plans, and if possible, you need more than one good plan to give you an exit strategy.

A deal might not work out. Plan A might not work out where you can make the money you wanted to make. Sometimes that happens and that's okay if you have a plan B, plan C, plan D where you can at least get out of the deal, maybe make a little money, maybe just get out and move on. Lesson learned.

Go find another deal, a better deal. The worst thing to do is have time and money tied up in something that you cannot get out of. That will kill you. It will kill all your momentum. It'll just rob the joy out of doing something like this. It'll set you back.

Boil all this down. Have a plan to get out before you even start getting in. Do it. Have the end in mind before you even start on the beginning. I don't know how to say that any simpler, but that is so critical. Understand that your plans can, and often do, get changed. And keep your eyes open to different and better exit plans after you get into the deal.

Chapter 9 – Tear it Apart - Walk the Property

I made a video on this same subject immediately after getting back in the truck after walking a 40-acre tract we just closed on. It was one of the 12 deals used as examples for this book. I was putting some finishing touches on the plan (see Chapter 7) we had to divide it up and resell it.

This is a 40-acre timberland tract. It has blacktop road frontage. It has available electricity and water, so it's a perfect tract to divide up to resell into small home sites. I wasn't going to do a subdivision. I hate doing subdivisions, but that's a different topic. My original plan was to divide it into four 10-acre tracts. With road frontage and utilities. They'd likely sell well.

I needed to walk it thoroughly and kind of tear it apart. If you've been listening to any of my videos, you know when I say "tear a tract apart," that means go look at it, learn everything you can about it, top to bottom, east to west. Just dig into it and find out all the nitty gritty. It's a good thing I did that, because on paper, it divides up into four 10-acre parcels. Square 40, divide it, survey it out, four rectangle tracts. Easy. But when you get out there and you stomp around on it and you walked the creek and you walk through those thickets and you get in that timber and look, it's really only going to divide into three good home site parcels.

The topography is such that when you get out there and get the ground under your boots and stomp around and follow all the details out, it just makes sense to have three home site tracts on this. So that's how I'm going to have it surveyed. Instead of four 10-acre parcels there, I'm going to have the north side of the road divided in half, and then the whole south side of the road as the third parcel.

So, it'll be about an 8 or 9 acre parcel, a 10 or 11 acre parcel, and then about 19 or 20 acres on the other side. It's three parcels instead of four, but they'll have excellent home site locations all on good, high ground, good ridges. And that'll be the best way to do it.

If I hadn't gone out there and walked it out thoroughly, following that creek out, and really digging into it, I would have had it surveyed into four 10-acre parcels that would still just accommodate three home site locations.

Buyers would likely walk those 10-acre parcels and learn that one wasn't suitable. So, by taking the time to do the hard work of walking it out in the middle of a Louisiana summer, I saved myself some money, some aggravation, and likely some time. You've got to do that to maximize the benefits of your plan.

Some people take shortcuts. They don't look at tracts at all. They buy "sight unseen" as I've mentioned in another chapter. Some people buy tracts just by riding down the road looking at it from their windshield. Some tracts you honestly can do that, but if you're not seeing everything from the windshield, you have to get your rear-end out there on the ground. And sometimes that is hard doing, especially some of the country we deal with and timberland tracts in the summer. It can get gnarly and nasty. The briars are thick, the rattlesnakes and cottonmouths are out. You got to get out there and stomp it out and tear it apart to maximize the tract and to know what problems you have so you can solve them.

You need to be able to solve the problems on the front end – in your plan - otherwise you'll be forever trying to sell that tract. You can't depend on just hoping that buyers won't notice the problems. They're going to notice and they're just going to move on to something else.

Solve the problems on the front end, the ones that you can. Know how to maximize the tracts so you can know what improvements to make, how much money to spend. And the only way to do that is to get the thing under your boots and walk it, feel it, tear it apart. It's hard work, especially when you're an old fat boy like me in a Louisiana summer. But that's the difference between making some decent money and making mistakes, spending too much money on a tract and not maximizing it. So, tear them apart, figure out the best plan, then go do your plan.

Chapter 10 – Stick with It

One of the 12 deals was 46 acres. It was just a normal day in, day out kind of tract that we try to buy and sell. The thing about this one is it took 16 months to close. From start to finish, 16 months, and that's me being on top of it the whole time!

The most important thing you must have to do land deals is not always a bunch of money. It is not luck. It is not always being at the right place at the right time. You must have the ability to stick with it. I promise you. I have patience, I can follow up, be kind and patient again and again, then follow up some more, and stay kind and keep your cool through the whole process.

It's going to be worth some money to you to be able to do that because things don't go smoothly when you're dealing with other people. I assure you they don't. There are 100 little hurdles you sometimes must jump through on these deals. Some of them go easy and quick, but then some like this one takes 16 months, and there were no major hurdles to overcome like title issues, boundary disputes, etc. That's the irritating part about it. It just took that long for 4 family members to work through the deal, to sign off on everything, to agree to this, to agree to that, then finally got around to moving forward. We were finally able to get a contract signed so we could get the survey done and the title work finished. Then the title company had to pick up where we left off and get all the family members' personal information and signatures on the closing documents. 16 months. I know it shouldn't take that long, but it did.

When you're dealing with deals where you have multiple people involved, some are estranged family members, they all live in different places, not all use email, and they all must make up their minds and get on the same page and agree...it can take a long time!

If and when they do finally agree, they all have to sign documents. They all have to FedEx. They all have to check their email. It just gets complicated sometimes keeping people on track. And not every kind of title company is created equal, either. Some of them really get moving and try to get things done because they know nothing happens until a deal closes. They really try to push for the closing and get everything done. Others just diddle along and take their time.

You must have patience and kindness and a little flex in a deal to be able to make it work. I could've gotten mad after a few months of this dragging on and said, "Hey, send that stuff now, or I'm done." Well, I could've done that. I'd probably have missed a great deal as a result. I was able to just stay involved, keep pushing and prodding gently, but being kind so I wouldn't tick anybody off, make anybody mad, and work with everybody to get it all done.

I got it done, and it's a good deal. We're going to do well on it. It's a cool property. It's 46 acres, part pasture, part bottomland hardwood. It's got blacktop road frontage, water, and electricity. It's in a desirable location. It's a great rural home site tract. I'm glad it's done. But, without the patience, without the ability to stick it through, I would have missed the deal.

There are a lot of people who have missed these deals because they think it's too much trouble. They think it ought to just be 1, 2, 3, A, B, C, sign, done, and in/out. It just doesn't always work that way. You're dealing with people and real life, real situations, things going on. You just must be able to ebb and flow, flex, and make it all kind of melt together and work together and hopefully come out at the end with the deal done. You'll find that some deals go quickly, and some go ridiculously slow. The slow ones, if you'll stick with them, could be the most rewarding at the end.

Chapter 11 – To Survey or Not to Survey

One of the properties in our list of 12 was about 50 acres. It was part pasture and part bottomland hardwood timber. I wanted to get it surveyed. I didn't have to get it surveyed to buy it. The legal descriptions were clear and solid.

The surveyor was just doing a straight boundary survey. That is just simply roping the property off. That's just my language for a boundary survey that creates the red lines you see on aerial plats, creates a complete mete and bounds (direction and distance) legal description, and certifies the exact acreage within the corners.

What it will also do is identify any encroachments that may be on the property. There's some fencing along three or four sides of the tract. It's sort of an odd shape so there's more than four sides. The survey will identify any fencing and tell me if the fencing is creeping in on the property we're buying or if our boundary falls short of where the fencing is. I'll tell you why that's important in just a second. It'll also identify any other things on the tract like any road or trails that cross the corners of it or go along the boundaries of the property that may zig zag on and off the tract. I don't think there were any on this tract, but a survey would identify all of that.

The survey doesn't fix those problems. It simply identifies them, and it creates a geographical snapshot, as I like to call it. A certified geographical snapshot, meaning whatever is going on on that tract at that time like fences, pipeline right of ways, power lines, any roads or trails that are going across the property, a neighbor's building, etc. It will identify those things and show officially where they are so that it can be argued in the future what was going on exactly in this moment in time. That's important for a number of reasons.

I met with him for another reason. I wanted him to do a little bit more than just the boundary survey. This surveyor is used to me asking him to create additional points-on-line between the corners. I ask him to put in points along a line between two corners and mark them with metal t-posts so they can be seen easier.

These additional points are handy along a line. When we go in and mark that boundary, which we often do because a lot of this is in timberland, we're compassing in and flagging from point to point, and it's a lot easier to do when you have more points to connect. It keeps you on course a lot easier than having to go from one corner all the way to the next corner which if often a quarter or half mile or longer in our business. Having additional points along the way that you can flag to and compass allow you to see and correct your line as you go in small segments. It makes it a lot easier than doing it all in one long line with just two points. At least it does to me.

You may be asking, "Pat, why not just have the surveyor mark and paint those boundary lines for you?" The short answer is the cost for the additional time. Sometimes we pay to have that done. Other times it's more cost effective to do it ourselves. Remember, our goal is to keep costs as manageable as possible so we can sell for as much profit as possible.

Anyway, back to this project. I had him add the points-on-line in some places. I also wanted him to identify some fencing, because our property line and some of those points went all the way up to the fence and beyond it which means that fence is encroaching on the property we're buying just a little bit. There were other places where the boundary line as he surveyed it was short of where the fence was. This meant, theoretically, the property between the surveyed boundary line and that fence, could be maintained, occupied, and claimed going forward. There's a lot more to it than that, don't get me wrong.

Nobody's stealing from me and I'm stealing from anyone. But when you have fences on the ground that have been there a long time, they typically become established property lines and it's good to know if you're gaining acres or losing acres if you use those fences as possession inside or outside a property line. That's a different conversation, but the survey capturing precisely where everything is at a specific time in history is important with regard to encroachments and possession issues.

Did you know that getting a survey on a tract you're buying gives you a little more teeth in your title policy if you get an owner's policy on a property? Having a survey takes one of the exceptions and exclusions out of that title policy and they can then insure, that's what a title policy does, that title as defined by that survey. That's helpful to you as well. Ask your title company about that.

When you're looking at property to buy, don't just automatically blow off the survey   just because you're in a state that doesn't require a survey to define a specific tract. The Public Land Survey System (PLSS) is used in many states. It was created by the Land Ordinance in 1785. They use the rectangular survey system that blocks land off by townships, ranges, and sections. Other states use a metes and bounds survey system to create geographical boundaries. Read about this sometime to understand how your state uses these methods. Here's a good place to start.

My point is to encourage you to just not blow it off just because you're not absolutely required to get it. Think through it like this: What am I going to use this property for? What is around me? What are some of the things on the ground either on or near my property that I want to identify as potential problems? Then ask yourself if it's just the money for the survey that is preventing you? Are you being so tight with money now on a project that has a likelihood of ending up costing you money in the future with some issues that you can see? As for me, as I've gotten older, I tend to err on the side of the survey. I don't get them all the time by any means but more often than not I'm adding in the survey cost as part of my plan for a tract.

The survey, on many tracts, gives me some peace of mind, and that peace of mind is worth something. Don't just nickel and dime your way through land deals. Try to be smart and think about the future in the deal. And especially if it's the size or type of tract that a foul up is going to be very expensive. Or if it's really small and the universe has gotten so tight around a piece of property you're buying that it very well could a fence, a swimming pool, a retaining wall, a shed, etc. comes into play because properties are so close now as there are more and more improved properties. Civilization is sort of becoming more asphalt and less green. Properties are closer and closer and tighter and tighter. So, think through those scenarios.

We bought a two hundred plus acre tract several years ago. I had this property surveyed and found out a barn on the neighbor's property had a corner that was crossing the edge of our property line. I remember it was seven feet across the property line, and it was just the corner of the building angling across our property line. That doesn't sound like much when you're dealing with almost 300 acres, but it needed to be addressed. The survey revealed a problem, and we had an easy solution for it. The neighbor is happy, and we're happy. Future landowners there will not have problems left over from our deal that will cause them problems...and the barn is still there!

My point about surveys for rural land tracts is the older I get and the more deals I do, I'm finding they're definitely worth it. I don't get surveys every time, there are exceptions. I may not get a survey but be sure to know that I think about it every time and make the best decision I can.

Just FYI...I speak about surveys in many videos and in our other books. I remember one of my early videos, and one with a lot of views, was about having points-on-line added on a large tract we were dividing and selling. Other videos give detailed reasons why we chose to survey specific tracts.

Chapter 12 – You Got the Survey - Now Follow Up.

I always go see a property after I have it surveyed. It allows me to see how actual boundaries and corners lay on the ground, in real life, just like buyers will see it when I try to sell it to them. It always helps me to see what kind of challenges I may have if my plan is to flag a line using points-on-line (see Chapter 11) I requested. Seeing actual survey work on the ground helps me see exactly where lines will hit roads, trails, and creeks, too. This matters when you may be planning improvements on a tract or planning to divide it.

There were two specific tracts among the 12 where the survey, and following up, and seeing the work on the ground, seemed important enough to talk about with you.

The first tract wasn't surveyed because I was uncomfortable with the acreage. I felt very comfortable with the legal description, and when I mapped it out on mapping software that we use, I felt real comfortable that it was right at the acreage I was anticipating. I had it surveyed because it was an old property. It hadn't changed hands in forever, and it was surrounded by three different owners with a highway on the fourth side. There were no markings on the ground to help identify the boundary lines with the three private-owner neighbors.

When we put this tract on the market, the next guy that comes along to buy it probably will not be in the business like I am. He's going to want to know and see exactly where his lines and corners are. I had it surveyed for that reason.

So, after the survey was complete, I made another trip to the tract to check it out. It was just great. It laid in there just like I thought it would. I had all the boundary lines blazed on this tract. A lot of times I don't do that. I sometimes mark the lines myself once the survey is done. Remember Chapter 10? I had the surveyor blaze the lines on this one because it was such rugged ground. Lines ran through a nasty creek bottom and some thickets and to be honest, I didn't want to have to go fight that. I'm a fat boy and it was summer in Louisiana. Following up on this survey gave me confidence I had no issues with anything along the boundary lines, and the boundary hit the highway right-of-way just like I'd hoped.

The second example was from a tract I had surveyed because I didn't feel comfortable with the acreage. I didn't feel comfortable with the legal description either. It was a 93-year-old legal description. A lot of things have changed over 93 years, including technology in the survey world. So, I had it surveyed. It was a good thing I did. The surveyor worked on it for about two solid weeks. He worked on the ground, in the courthouse pulling old deeds, and in his office deciphering all of it. It was a mess. It turned out to be the acreage was about what we anticipated it being, but the markings on the ground with the adjoining landowners were off considerably. The new survey put new lines on the ground, got a rock-solid legal description and made this tract much more marketable.

If I had bought that property the way it was and then tried to resell it, I probably would end up with a mess with the next buyer. The lines were wrong on the ground and the legal description was funky. (Yea, funky can be used a real estate term.) This new survey, even though it was going to be a little bit expensive, was worth the money on this deal to get all that corrected.

Surveys are expensive. It's important we get what we're looking for when we pay to have them done. Following up on your surveys to ensure your goals and objectives are met is important.

As you'll know if you read Chapter 10 or seen any of our videos on surveys, I don't always get a survey. The older I get, however, the more deals I do, the more likely I am to buy survey work. It helps eliminates a lot of issues. A little bit of money to alleviate a lot of grief, pain, issues, and problems, when you get my age, you get as busy as we are, is money well spent. And go back and check the work!

Chapter 13 – Get it Closed

Nothing can happen until you get the deal closed. That could literally be the whole chapter there.

But let's expand the idea. Doing real estate deals is a lot more than everyone happily signing a few papers and running to their respective banks to deposit big checks. Deals can – and do! - get complicated. You're dealing with people. You're dealing with chains of title that may be dozens of years old. You're dealing with legal descriptions that are decades old. You're dealing with multiple people, multiple personalities, attorneys, abstracters, appraisers, surveyors, lenders... the list goes on and on.

All of the people involved in your deal have to do their part. They all must do their part correctly and timely for it to all come together to get a closing whether you're buying or selling. Sometimes people mess up, sometimes people aren't on the same time schedule you're on, often people just don't give a rip. You've got to understand that there's always going to be problems getting a deal across the finish line. You've just got to stick to it and keep it moving along.

The main thing about real estate is just solving problems and to do that, you've just got to stick with it and address each problem or roadblock as it comes up.

A skill to develop is knowing when to be patient. I'm not all that patient by nature. It's just I've done this enough you know that you sometimes have to roll with the punches. Sometimes you've just got to be sweet even though you know you've got every right in the world to be mad and upset. But you've just got to stay at an even keel and deal with it, because at the end of the day, you want people to work with you and to help you. Anything you do to assist that is going to make a difference, I promise.

At the time of developing this chapter, I had three deals in various stages of closing that were wearing on my patience. One property required a succession to be completed by the sellers before they could complete the sale to me. The lack of proper succession was discovered by the closing attorney when he did the title search. This meant the people selling the property to me were not – yet – the official successors in title and could not complete the sale.

They had gotten a property willed to them, but just because it's willed to you, doesn't mean that you are the successor in title until the succession is done and a judgment of possession is rendered. All that said, it had to be done and that took several weeks to do. During that additional time, I'm thinking of all the ways the family members could come up with ways to sink the deal. And to make things worse, I already had a buyer for this tract!

I couldn't complete the sale to my buyer until I closed the sale with the current owners – who weren't really the owners yet because the succession hadn't been done! I just knew my buyer was going to get tired of waiting and move on.

It all held together, and it finally got done. I regularly touched base with the attorney to kindly and gently keep everybody prodded along until the family completed the succession and was able to close their deal with me. I then turned around the next week and sold it and made decent money by just sticking with it.

One of the other tracts I was struggling to get closed was on a property that I was able to get a quick sale on. I got a contract, and it was moving along. We're going to do really well on this, but the lender for the buyer is asking for an extension. Okay, that's not unusual, but this is the third extension and there have been two amendments. I've amended the contract twice to account for the additional time needed, and I had to extended it for the third time. At some point it's easy to just say, "To heck with it. If you're not going to close, we're done. I'm not extending it."

Well, let's slow down and take a look. We're way down the track on this deal. I know that the buyers can get this done. It's not a credit issue. It's not a buyer issue. It's a lender issue. The lender's timetable is just not our timetable. They think the world revolves around them and they could just drag their feet and get it done whenever they want to regardless of what the contracted closing date stipulates.

I've given a little with these extensions, because I know in the next week or so, we'll have this closing, and it will all be worth it. That's why on those kinds of deals I just bite my tongue and go, "Hey, no problem." Another week is another week, but I don't want to wreck a good deal over a principle that I will not extend the contract for another short period.

If I just wanted to stand on principle, that'd be great, but I'd have a lot of unsold properties. There are times to give, then there are times to stand firm. This is one of those times to give a little.

The third closing was just a matter of getting all the cats herded. There were no issues to solve other than gathering all the signatures. I touched base with the closing attorney to ask him where the deal was. I asked, "Hey, just touching base. I want to see where our deal is." We, as buyers, have already signed and put our money in the closing attorney's escrow. The closing attorney has sent the documents out to the five sellers for their signatures. Five sets of documents emailed to five different people in five different places.

All five agreed to sell. They all signed the contract. They all signed an extension that the attorney asked for a few weeks ago. Everybody signed, but still at the end of the day, you wait to get all these signatures back to get it done. Because until everybody signs, all five of them, you don't have a deal. Four of them signed and returned the documents right away, but the fifth one decided to leave the documents at home and take their trip to the beach before they would meet with a notary and execute the documents. That was a 10-day trip!

We spent real money on this deal. We have spent money on the survey. I've got a lot of time in this deal, and at the end of the day I'm still waiting to get it signed by one of the sellers to have an official sale.

Those are just three scenarios that arise with closings. There are many other tales of woe that I could write but you get the point. There are things you've just got to deal with, and the way to do it, is to sit down and send an email, or pick up your phone, make a call, be kind, be clear, be brief, but keep prodding people along. Do it in a professional, encouraging, and nice way. You've got to be firm at times, but you never want to just go scorched earth and blow a deal, blow relationships, blow your reputation, just because something isn't going just right or moving at the pace you prefer.

Stick with the deal. Don't hide from issues or problems hoping they'll just work themselves out. Don't sit back letting weeks roll by without finding out what's going on with the professionals (attorneys, surveyors, lenders, appraisers, etc.) whom you depend on to get their part of the deals done. Get your closings across the finish line so you can execute your plans and make some money.

Chapter 14 – Add Acreage to Maximize Value

Let's talk about a sure-fire way to minimize the cost of your expenses by diluting it over more acreage. You can find adjoining tracts to buy to help you improve your deal.

This idea crystalized in my mind when I got some news on a piece of property that we were trying to buy. It joined a tract that we already owned that had an access issue. We were solving the access issue by purchasing an access from the adjoining neighbor.

Well, that access costs money. We had to survey the access route. We had to pay the adjoining owner a fee for his granting that access to us. We had some legal work with fees. It all added up to several thousand dollars just for the access. That would become a fixed expense as it related to the tract we owned. But the tract that was landlocked directly behind ours would benefit from that access if I could buy it.

The point in this is I'm maximizing the value of my improvements. I'm maximizing the value of the expenses. I had to spend money to buy the access for our tract. That's already done, and I was willing to do that. I had already pulled the trigger on it. Now I can add some acres to that tract that'll utilize the same access that I've already paid for. So that money is already spent, but now I can spread that expense out over more acres. That's a no-brainer. I'd absolutely want to do that.

We can buy this small tract over here, add it to our existing tract, make it bigger, and now everything has legal access. And as a bonus, the additional tract I purchased was bought at a very reasonable price because it didn't have a deeded access. I could then sell it with my tract at a higher price now that it did have an access.

You might be making other improvements other than access that you can then spread the cost over more acres and maximize your profits when you sell.

Keep diluting that cost out over more acres as long as the deal doesn't get too big or too unmanageable for you. The deal is getting better all the time as the expenses for improvements stay the same, or increase only slightly, but the acreage grows. Those kinds of opportunities can take one of your ho-hum, average, run-of-the-mill deals and turn it into a homerun.

Keep your eyes open for this kind of opportunity around properties you own or about to close on.

Chapter 15 – Make the Right Improvements

Let's consider a 30-acre tract to discuss simple improvements. I bought this tract after the timber was clear cut. All that was left were some scattered, small oak trees and an occasional, very large pine that was too limby and gnarly to have any saw timber value.

The tract was long and narrow and was divided by a parish road. Parish is a Louisiana county!

We paid a good bit for the tract being a clear cut in a very rural area. I knew we were going to do well after I finished a couple projects on it.

Now, let's pause for a second to discuss improvements. I don't want you to get the wrong ideas here. I'm not discussing a site prep job for a multi-use urban project. Nor am I talking about adding all the infrastructure for a 300-home subdivision. Remember that we're discussing rural real estate. The improvements I'll discuss here are the basics for making a small or mid-sized rural tract more desirable to the average buyer.

I already had this place surveyed. I did that as part of the purchase, and we paid for it by the final surveyed acre. The survey was important on the front end before the purchase, but it was also part of the improvement plan. While getting a boundary survey to determine the exact acreage and to locate any encroachments along the boundaries (See Chapter 11), I had the surveyor divide the tract into three different parcels. These three parcels would be marketed separately. Remember from Chapter 11 that it's easier and cheaper to have this extra work done at the same time your boundary survey is being done. This type of efficiency will save you a lot of time and money, but it's only possible if you already have your plan thought out before you close (See Chapter 8).

The survey and the commitment to divide the tract into 3 parcels was the first improvement. When a buyer can see a recent survey plat and legal description of a parcel you want to sell, believe me, that's considered an improvement!

The second simple improvement was to hire a bulldozer operator. I had used this same gentleman a few times prior, so his rate and quality of work was not something I had to investigate. It pays to develop good relationships with people who can provide the services you need on your properties. Find good people and stick with them. The loyalty is way more valuable than having to shop around all the time because you always want the cheapest instead of the most reliable. Reliable wins over discount every time.

I had the dozer operator come spend several days pushing up into large piles all the debris, the slash, the stumps, the limbs etc. created by the past timber harvest.   Just pushing it all up in piles would allow me to burn it easier as well as open up the ground so people could see the tract better.

I didn't have him clear up all 30 acres. No, I just cleared up maybe two to three acres on the road frontage on both sides of the road. We planned to sell parcels on both sides of the road as well as third parcel across a creek on the far end of the second parcel.

Just clearing up the road frontage a little bit will allow people to visualize a nice rural home site location when they see it. They'll see great road frontage, available utilities, high rolling ground in a cool part of the country. They'll be able to see what a home site could look like because it had been cleaned up.

I've learned it's always better when you can take little bit of the imagination factor off the table for some potential buyers. You don't have to sell them on what it can look like, they can drive right out there and see for themselves. This does part of the sales work for you.

I spent a few thousand dollars for the dozer work and cleaning up the two larger road frontage parcels. Let's look at improvement number three.

The final step in my improvement plan was to secure approximately 50 feet to be able to access the third parcel from another public road it very nearly touched. I had this access point surveyed in my original survey, because I knew I'd need it at some point. I had the dozer guy clean part of this smaller parcel up so I could show the adjacent landowner how the access would connect my property to the road. Everything was going according to plan until...

That's right. The adjoining neighbor has been unwilling to sell us that small strip. I don't know why. He just has been unwilling up to this point. I am still working on that final phase of the plan for this tract. I never said all this easily worked every time.

Fortunately, this final parcel is only about four acres of the total deal. We quickly sold the larger two parcels and made very good money. These four acres are just sitting there. It will eventually work out and we'll make some bonus money when we can sell it with the access. The two – and hopefully the third! – basic improvements turned a deal into a home run.

I discussed a lot of improvements that can help rural land deals sell quicker and for more money in my first land book, How to Sell Your Land Faster. Check it out for more ideas. Here you were encouraged to make necessary improvements to improve value and desirability. Don't be afraid to make reasonable improvements so long as you are sure it will result in being able to sell the land for more money per acre or sell it much faster. Be sure your improvements fit the type tract you're dealing with and are reflective of the area. Don't put a gold ring in a pig's nose!

Chapter 16 – When it is OK to NOT Make Money on a Deal

Let's switch gears just a bit and discuss something that is a little less tactical. I want to give you my opinion on something that may or may not suit you. I recommend this for people who have done several deals successfully. They know what they're doing, and they've got a risk tolerance already established. This is for people who understand in general, what different types of land is selling for in their region. They've got more than just a basic level of information or knowledge base. Let's call them an advanced investor just for conversation.

That doesn't mean they're some expert. It just means they've got some experience. One of the deals in this 12, was a deal where I did it strictly to learn something. That was more important in the deal than making money. That doesn't mean that I did not want to make money on it. In fact, my plan was to make money but that was secondary to what I wanted to learn. And I was willing to lose some money to learn if it came down to that.

The property was small. It was 20 acres of woodlands and recreational land in the Midwest. I had never bought anything in this area before. I gathered a little information on general values in the area and made an offer that I thought would still allow me to flip it for a small profit. The seller said he'd take it. So, now I owned the 20 acres and my learning could begin.

My exit strategy was to just put it right back on the market without doing any work on it or spending any extra money on improvements. Hopefully I could get a deal for $300-400 an acre more and get out. That was plan 'A'. But even more important as making money, I wanted to learn something about land value in this area. I wanted to understand the process and how area title companies worked. I wanted to learn how people responded to tracts like this and the price point I was using. I wanted to see how long these smaller tracts took to get serious interest.

I was taking a small risk to learn a lot because I could take that information going forward and apply it to bigger deals and make money on those. So, in my mind, my doing this deal was an investment in my real estate education for this new part of the country. I had calculated that it would be worth just breaking even or even losing a little if I'd overpaid for this tract.

Anyway, after closing on the deal I put it right back on the market. I changed the advertising just a little. The short story is I sold the tract in less than two months for a little over six thousand dollars more. Now six thousand dollars doesn't sound like a lot of money. But on a $20,000 deal in less than two months, when you're expecting just to break even at best, that's not too bad. That's a great rate of return. I don't care how you calculate it, that's a good ROI. I'd take those deals all day long.

So, it worked out great. I made a little money and I learned what I wanted to learn. Now that same information that I learned on a little 20-acre tract can be applied to bigger tracts and make larger chunks of cash in the future. Even if I didn't make a dime, that was money and time well spent.

This may not work for you. But I learn that way. I've got so many deals going on, and we're so busy with RecLand, that if I don't have means or reason to deeply engage with a property, I'll miss out on the details. Properties will fly by me and I'm not going to learn what I need to learn. I knew when I put money at risk, however, that it would have my attention. I knew that I would be engaged in it and would pay attention to the details as we went along, and I would learn what I needed to learn. That's how I do it. I must have my fingers in the pie and feel it to know what it's all about.

Now I could've studied a bunch of comparable sales and talked to a lot of people. I could've made a lot of phone calls, asked a lot of questions and probably gotten a general idea of what I learned by actually doing this land deal. But when I put my money up and engage in it, those lessons are mine. I have them. I learned them...they are mine. Investing a few months and some money provided all this information to me for certain tracts in that part of the country. Now if another deal comes along, I won't have to do a whole lot of research or a whole lot of thinking. I can confidently pull the trigger and make a deal.

If you get to the point where you have some comfort level in your market in terms of understanding pricing to the degree you know that you can't get hurt on a deal, you may want to broaden your experience by dabbling in some new areas or new type tracts. Use your experience to limit your risks, but don't be afraid to miss your ROI goals on some deals in an effort to learn new things and stretch your capabilities. Don't look at it as loss but as the price for new information and experience in different geographies, different types of land, different uses of parcels, etc. That can be money well spent because that information may can be parlayed it into bigger deals down the road, and that information will make you some money.

The same thing applies to a tract we already own in East Texas. It was not part of the 12 deals that are the basis for this book. This parcel was part of a much bigger package our investment group bought. My plan was to clear cut the timber then clear the ground to create small home site tracts as mini-ranches.

I planned to spend the money to have the stumps removed and all the debris piled and burned so the tract could be converted to pasture ground for livestock. The cost of dozer and track hoe work would be quite a bit, but it wasn't so much that it made the project risky. We may not be able to sell the parcels at what I hoped to make a good profit. I felt that worst case would be selling it for enough to at least get our improvement costs back.

It was a mini-experiment to test the market for these mini-ranches in this area. If it worked, I could then feel confident I could repeat the project again and again. If it didn't turn out as I planned, then my risk and exposure was limited to just this 60-acre deal. It's better to learn on 60 acres than on 6000, in my opinion! There are less zeros involved in the dollars!

So, we're going to spend a chunk of money to learn something. I encourage you to get to the point where your comfort level, experience level, and risk tolerance level will allow you to do some deals to learn something that you can then apply to future deals to make more money. And if you go about it just right, you'll learn something and make money!

Chapter 17 – The Recap

Have you noticed that we've gotten his far and I haven't dedicated much space to how to sell your tract for a profit? The reason is that so many of the little steps to selling are baked in the searching, work, planning, evaluating, and improving a property you bought that we discussed in the previous chapters. The actual process of selling is occurring all along the way if you've done your work and not tried to cut corners or follow the get-rich-quick schemes.

Once you've bought a property well and executed your plan – whether sophisticated or simple – you're almost home. Simply make a plan as to when and how you want to sell it.

Here are a couple little things to consider as you put your property on the market:

1. Use a pro. I'm a land broker so it goes without saying I believe you should hire a good land agent to represent your property and market it broadly. The thing about land tracts is that a buyer can come from anywhere in the world so use a land broker who can market widely. Don't get so cheap that you feel the 5-6% commission is too much of an expense. You can't advertise your tract as broadly as a top land broker can.

2. Be sure it's ready to go before turning on the "for sale" sign. Put your best foot forward so buyers will get a good first impression. Take a look at my book "How to Sell Your Land Faster" for lots of tips to get it ready.

3. Don't be greedy on the resale. Your experience in buying and improving the property should have given you a good idea of the retail market value for the tract. Make a plan to sell it around that number. Don't fall in love with your handiwork to the degree you get unrealistic with the value. Get an offer at or near the fair market value and SELL IT! Take the money, have a beer, congratulate yourself on your achievement whether small or great, and then move on to the next one.

4. Be looking for more deals while this one is on the shelf to sell. Be planning your next deal or deals.

I wanted to give you a little summary of how the 12 deals went to give you some perspective. As I've tried to communicate throughout this book, and all my other books and videos, honest land trading is not a get-rich-quick scheme that you just learn with someone's master program you bought online. It takes time and work. Sometimes you do well. Other times you take some lumps.

Overall, several of the 12 deals went great. They were in and out, easy, and we made good money per acre on them. A couple of the other deals have done well, too, they just took a little longer. There were two deals that were just so-so, ho-hum. Yea, we made some money on them, but they had some extra hassles and longer time frames that resulted in them being just little singles instead of doubles and triples. We learned things from these two deals that will add to the couple hundred bucks an acre we made and thereby making them worthwhile deals.

One deal is not complete yet. Well, in terms of selling all the acreage it's not yet complete. It's a 4-acre parcel that is at the end of 26 acres we already sold. The 26 acres were a home run in terms of profit, so sitting on these last four acres is hardly a burden. The four acres is just costing us about $12 per year in property taxes. It's not a burden! We are still working out the best way to get access to it so we can sell it for a nice chunk of change like we did the 26 acres that was part of it. It will then go in the "homerun" category.

That's the reality of trying to make money buying and selling land. If you do enough deals, you're going to hit some homers that make it seem like the easiest work in the world. Most of the time, however, you'll grind it out with singles and doubles and the occasional triple. You'll have to work to squeeze every dollar out of the deal. And to continue the sports metaphor, occasionally you'll just lose one. Everything will go wrong, and you'll just have to take your L and get ready for the next one. The key to the L's is learn something so you don't have to experience those problems or mistakes the next time.

So, set aside all those "no work," "no risk," "no money required" notions and master seminars and go find a deal. Do the work to figure out what you must do to make money with it. Study it, walk it, plan it, work it, critique it, see it, and then put up some real money and get busy making money by buying and selling land.

Let me know how you do!

Bonus Chapter

Due Diligence – Some Additional Items to Check before Buying Rural Land

By Pat Porter

From "Land Buying Tips from the Pros – How to Buy Rural Real Estate" available in ebook, paperback & audio at Amazon.

I looked up the definition of due diligence in several different places and found these recurring words: investigation, analysis, research, reasonable, certainty and confirmation. These are heavy words that carry a lot of responsibility. And all this responsibility falls squarely on the shoulders of you, the buyer, when you plan to buy land.

No one will care about the details of the deal any more than you. Doing your due diligence can save you a lot of future heartache and money on that land tract you're about to buy. In this short chapter, I'll outline several key areas, in addition to the usual things most people check when buying real estate that will get you thinking about what else to check and verify on your next rural real estate purchase.

The Purchase Contract

Due diligence starts with the purchase contract. Read it, understand it, ask questions about it, and use it to fully detail the terms of the purchase as they have been negotiated with the seller. Your land agent should be diligent to help you document the terms of the deal clearly in the purchase contract. Having the seller and buyer see "eye to eye" on the terms at this stage of the deal will reduce the chances of something going wrong for either party before closing. Regardless of how well things seem to be going at this stage, get all the verbal agreements written into the contract. Even the best of intentions can fall prey to bad memories and misunderstandings later.

Remember, a purchase contract by its design will capture all the big items in a deal that rarely cause the problems. Things like purchase price, closing date, and legal description won't usually be an issue later on. It's the smaller things that creep up and bugger up a deal (yea, "bugger up" is a real estate term). Get those smaller details on paper at the beginning.

Existing Easements & Leases

Depending on the present use of the land, you will need to verify any number of items that will affect your future use of the tract. Have you seen the CRP or WRP contracts that are still in place on the tract? Have you read the restrictions of the conservation easement, the deed restrictions, timber reservations, or other encumbrances that will limit the use of the tract? Have you, or your attorney seen and read them? What about that hunting lease or farm lease...does it match what you were told during the negotiating process? Ask to see the conveyance document on "deeded accesses" if you are depending on it for your supposed legal access.

All the above contracts and leases are available either as recorded documents in your county or parish records (these are public information), the local Farm Service Agency (you'll need the landowner's permission to get copies here), or available from the current owner. Be sure your written purchase agreement has language that says the seller has provided you with a copy of any lease, easement, or agreement that may not be found in the public records.

Here's an example of how this type follow up saved a large acreage deal. I was helping a group of buyers purchase nearly 2000 acres of bottomland that was purely a recreational tract. They knew they weren't getting the mineral rights since those rights were already under lease, and the tract had a number of producing gas wells on it. They were concerned, however, that all the coming and going of the gas company would be a problem for them when trying to divide the tract and sell parcels to hunters. After all, who wants to spend a bunch of money on a place to deer hunt and then have people riding through your property at 9 a.m. checking a gas well?

I found out who the gas company was and made a call. I was able to speak with the field supervisor for that area and that tract. He told me they had a policy about limiting property visits during hunting season and trying to come only during the middle of the day when it was necessary.

This piece of information eased the buyers' minds and they bought the tract. Their re-sell efforts were also successful since this little bit of information was enough to make the original concern a non-issue. But they wouldn't have known without the additional phone call. And it's the kind of phone call and follow up that isn't part of the closing attorney's general checklist of things to do. You must do this kind of checking for yourself.

Wetlands

If you plan to clear some of the tract for farming, development, or even a new road, will you be clearing wetlands? You don't know until you've seen a wetland determination report. Will that bridge you need require a 404 Permit from the Corps of Engineers or expensive mitigation credits?

Go to the Corps website at www.usace.army.mil and click on the link "Find a Corp Office" to get the office in your area. You'll find there are 30-40 offices in the United States with most of them located in the eastern half of the country. Call and ask if you're not certain.

"But Pat, I'll be opening up a can of worms if I call them!" I hear you…and tend to agree a little bit. But you could be opening a can of snakes – in the form of expensive litigation and after-the-fact remedies – if you don't check before you begin an expensive, or expansive project. Our experience has shown that these folks will just guide you to perform only what's necessary as your project impacts wetlands, streams, etc. and leave you alone if your plans don't otherwise cross into these type problem areas.

If in doubt...call them before you buy.

Environmental Issues

Diligent buyers of farmland look for large diesel spills at wells and near fuel tanks and check for empty chemical containers dumped in nearby ditches or creeks to alert them of potential environmental quality issues. A Phase 1 environmental evaluation is not a big deal to get, but it could turn into a big deal if you don't.

You can get good information about this from your state's Department of Environmental Quality. Simply Google Department of Environmental Quality for your state's particular website. They can direct you to local companies or consultants who can perform these checks for you.

Timber Markets

Timberland buyers should understand the area markets and mills if buying a tract in a new area. How far away are the area mills and what type of wood product are they taking? Will the terrain allow complete mechanical harvest or are there acres that loggers just won't be able to work? This can be a costly thing to find out later if you put a considerable value on that timber in those unworkable areas. Do you have good access to get your timber out? Not all timber markets are the same. Not all timber tracts are the same, either. Consulting a local forester in an area you're new in may prevent a costly mistake.

Title, Mineral, Groundwater Checks

Your closing attorney should be able to catch title issues that may cause you problems if left uncured, but you may need to specify that he look for items that are critical to your reason for purchase. For instance, if you're buying half the mineral rights, does that mean half of 100% or does the seller only own 50% herself and you're really just getting half of half? A general title search will not necessarily determine this information for you. If confirming this information is critical, you'll need to take the initiative to have a mineral abstract performed.

Just a word of caution about title searches. It could be helpful to you to be sure your attorney checks the title back further than a typical "30 years plus 1 chain" to pick up some old leases that may have been executed 40, 50 years ago, or longer. These leases exist. I've seen them, and I've seen this very issue create problems for buyers and sellers. A title policy can help reduce risks associated with title issues. We have a chapter devoted to title policies in this book. It's written by a practicing attorney specializing in real estate transactions. Be sure to read it.

If you are buying land in a state like Texas where groundwater can be reserved, you will want to know the status on your tract. Be sure to ask your attorney or title company.

Flood Plains and Access to River Tracts

You can verify river stages, flood histories, and FEMA flood plain data yourself online these days if the tract is in a marginal elevation area. But you need to do this. Ask your land agent to help you identify internet resources if you need them. Confirm the information you've been told if you're unsure. Ask your homeowners insurance agent to help you check the area where you may plan to build a home or a camp.

What river stage at the nearest upstream bridge does a rising river cut off use of the access road to your property? When was the last time it got this high...or how often?

Here's the best place to start if you want to investigate the federal database for floodplains in the US. Go to www.fema.gov. Click the Navigation tab on the left. Scroll down and click the Flood Map Service Center tab. This will take you to a page where you can enter the property's location, and the site will locate the flood plain map for that area. You'll see an overview of the flood zone designations. This is a good place to start especially if you have plans to build on the property.

The list of items to verify can go on and on depending on the tract and its use. The point is to confirm, verify, and understand all the major items that will impact you the hardest. Your land agent is required by law to tell you about all material facts he is aware of that may impact the property's value and use. The key is "that he is aware of." Your agent may not know everything about every detail that is critical to you. You as the buyer are ultimately responsible to satisfy and protect your future interests, to your satisfaction and level of comfort, with thoughtful due diligence.

About the Author

Pat Porter is the broker for RecLand Realty, LLC. His main office is in Monroe, Louisiana. His company site is www.RecLand.net and its video blog is www.RecLand.net/recland-news. RecLand has an active YouTube channel at https://www.youtube.com/reclandtalks. Feel free to email Pat at office@recland.net.

Thanks again! Please take a minute to see our other land-related books at https://www.amazon.com/Pat-Porter/e/B00LWUVMS6 and leave a review at Amazon for any of the books you read.

Wrapping It All Up

Thanks for reading my humble little book.

I hope you got an idea or two that will help you in your next land deal. The information provided here is the real deal. This isn't just a collection of ideas found in a Google search. This is how I personally do things.

There may have been other topics you wanted to see discussed. Maybe I can get to some of those another time. I'm always learning and trying to share what I learn. There are so many specific topics that can be covered since there is such a vast variety of land types, sizes, and uses all over our great country. We will keep trying to provide more information as we go in new books and videos.

Please take a minute to provide a review of my book. It just takes a second, and they are so valuable to us writers trying to make our material available to people online. I believe you got plenty of value for the cost in this deal so I would be grateful for your help in giving this book a little notice so it can be useful to others, too.

At RecLand Realty, all we do is land. Let us know when we can serve you. We can be found pretty easily by going to www.RecLand.net or our video blog at www.RecLand.net/recland-news. At the video blog, you will see dozens of short videos where I discuss land-related subjects as well as things associated with the RecLand brand. You can learn a lot of specific details about rural land there. Take a look at them and use the tags on each page to help you locate the videos and subjects you have interest in.

You can also find out what we're up to at www.facebook.com/recland and www.facebook.com/reclandtalks.   Check out our RecLand Talks YouTube channel and Instagram page. Just search RecLand or RecLandRealty and join us. We have 2 podcast shows RecLand Realty and RecLand Talks that can be found on all major podcast platforms. I am always accessible by email at office@recland.net.

Remember, this information is provided as-is and does not in any way make or imply any guarantees as to any outcome. You will need to evaluate the information herein and consult the appropriate professionals such as surveyors, attorneys, tax accountants or any other professional or agency to acquire the information and guidance you need to help you make any decision that is best for you.

Pat Porter, Broker.

RecLand Realty, LLC – 410 Olive Street – Monroe, LA 71201

Other rural real estate books by Pat Porter:

"How to Sell Your Land Faster – Proven Ways to Improve the Value & Desirability of Rural Land" **is available in ebook, paperback & audio at Amazon**

"The Stuff the Best Land Agents Do: And You Should Do Them, Too!" **is available in ebook & audio at Amazon**

"Land Buying Tips From the Pros – How to Buy Rural Real Estate" **is available in ebook, paperback & audio at Amazon**

"Land Mines: Lessons to Keep Your Rural Real Estate Deals from Blowing Up" **is available in ebook & audio at Amazon**

"Dumb Questions: Avoid Asking These Questions When You Are Buying Rural Real Estate" **is available in ebook & audio at Amazon**

"MORE Land Buying Tips from the Pros – How to Buy Rural Real Estate" **is available in ebook paperback & audio at Amazon**

Or just visit my author page at https://www.amazon.com/Pat-Porter/e/B00LWUVMS6 **to see them all in one place.**